Dad's Little
Instruction Book

Annie Pigeon

Dad's Little Instruction Book

P
PINNACLE BOOKS

PINNACLE BOOKS are published by

Kensington Publishing Corp.
850 Third Avenue
New York, NY 10022
http://www.pinnaclebooks.com

First Pinnacle Printing: June, 1995
10 9 8 7 6 5 4 3

ISBN: 0-7860-0150-X

Printed in the United States of America

1. Arrange for paternity leave.

2. Take power naps.

3. Get a jogging stroller.

4. Show the kids your scars.

5. Learn to clip your baby's fingernails.

6. Face it: your childless friends think you've gone off the deep end.

7. Make a frame for their artwork.

8. Teach them to read maps.

9. Teach them to tie knots.

10. Let them ride on your shoulders.

11. Let them ride on your bike seat.

12. Let them ride you like a horsie.

13. Tell them about the time you got stitches.

14. Always remember the punch line.

15. Show them how you tie your tie.

16. Find out just how to get a ship in a bottle.

17. Beg them not to say "My dad can beat up your dad."

18. Let your kids watch you shave.

19. Expose them to classical music—Dylan, the Beach Boys, and the Grateful Dead.

20. Learn to make pizza dough and flip it in the air.

21. (Or, learn to flip the phone in the air while you're ordering pizza.)

22. If Paul Newman can make spaghetti sauce, so can you.

23. While your wife is pregnant, you'll gain fifteen pounds.

24. Learn where the all-night pharmacy is.

25. Be an optimist.

26. Carve a pumpkin.

27. If Barbie has a sportscar, why can't you?

28. It's not enough to win the bread, you have to bake it too.

29. If you want a bathroom to yourself, build an outhouse.

30. Learn to juggle—your schedule, that is.

31. Tell your expectant wife, she's radiant.

32. Never argue with someone in her third trimester.

33. Pretend you can tell what's what in the sonogram.

34. Rub her tummy with cocoa butter to prevent stretch marks.

35. Help the kids look through a telescope.

36. Teach them to use a compass.

37. Educate.

38. Speculate.

39. Explain why bears hibernate.

40. Work on a jigsaw puzzle with them.

41. Teach them to follow your "tracks" in the snow.

42. Don't hog the train set.

43. Give them their own computer diskette.

44. Hook up a CD-Rom.

45. Point out the constellations.

46. Delegate.

47. Participate.

48. Negotiate.

49. Hug.

50. Mug.

51. Help them catch a lightning bug.

52. Build a model airplane together.

53. Know when to stop tickling.

54. Getting thrown up on is a badge of honor.

55. Help them find the North Star.

56. Talk to your baby in the womb so he'll get to know your voice.

57. The waiting room is for sissies.

58. The delivery room is where it's at.

59. Have long talks.

60. Take nature walks.

61. Real men wear rice cereal.

62. It's your turn to diaper.

63. It's your turn to rock.

64. Paisley ties conceal spit-up.

65. Wearing a Snugli is macho.

66. Pushing a stroller is macho.

67. Handing them to mommy when they cry is not macho.

68. Learn the names of all of Thomas the Tank Engine's friends.

69. It's another fine mess you've gotten yourself into.

70. Some bad news about fatherhood: you can't breastfeed.

71. Some good news about fatherhood: you can't breastfeed.

72. You weren't the first to faint during a circumcision.

73. When a baby's brand new you'll mostly want to just stare at it.

74. Buy your son his first baseball bat.

75. Ditto for your daughter.

76. Help break in the new catcher's mitt.

77. Tell your son it's O.K. to be sad.

78. Tell your daughter it's O.K. to be mad.

79. Teach your kids to save money.

80. Save some yourself.

81. Remind them: it's buy *low*, sell *high*.

82. Teach your kids how to whistle.

83. Teach your kids how to whittle.

84. Fax a note or drawing home from work.

85. Ask if it's okay to coach their team.

86. Help them think of neat surprises for Mom.

87. Let them beat you at arm wrestling.

88. Grill your daughter's dates.

89. Run a credit check on your future son-in-law.

90. O.K., so Ward Cleaver you're not.

91. O.K., so Iron John you're not either.

92. That "fire in your belly" means you ate too much chili.

93. Leave your work at the office.

94. Leave your mood at the office.

95. Attend all school plays.

96. Take the kids fly fishing.

97. Remember: fatherhood is a work in progress.

98. The most precious thing you can give your kids is time.

99. You don't always know best.

100. Have an answer ready for: did *you* drink beer?

101. Have an answer ready for: did you date anyone but Mom?

102. Have an answer ready for: did you inhale?

103. Teach your son all you know about women.

104. (Then think of something to fill the rest of the hour.)

105. Tell your daughter all you know about finding a good man.

106. (Then assure her they *do* still make them like you.)

107. Tell them part-time work builds character.

108. Remind them to shovel *your* driveway first.

109. Come out from behind that camcorder.

110. Board meetings are not the best time to show baby pix.

111. Coffee break is the best time to show baby pix.

112. It's O.K. to cry when you walk your daughter down the aisle.

113. It's also O.K. to cry when you get the catering bill.

114. Show them pictures of you as a child.

115. Bet you didn't know you could be such a pushover.

116. It's never too late to roller blade.

117. It's never too late to skateboard.

118. It's never too early to have a mid-life crisis.

119. Teach them how to keep score at baseball games.

120. Let out your Santa suit after Thanksgiving.

121. No, your kids can't have a boa constrictor.

122. No, neither can you.

123. No, they can't have a Harley Davidson.

124. No, neither can you.

125. Be encouraging.

126. Be realistic.

127. Don't act like an expert when you're not.

128. Remember, your wife's *their* mommy, not yours.

129. Take them to the National Air & Space Museum.

130. Station wagons are not macho.

131. Sports utility vehicles are mucho macho.

132. Stay in town for the parent teacher conference.

133. You too can have post-partum depression.

134. Don't knock daytime TV till you've tried it.

135. Have them learn to ski while they're still short.

136. Keep your promises.

137. Law of the Universe: some assembly is always required.

138. Law of the Universe: batteries are never included.

139. Do funny voices.

140. Make funny faces.

141. Read a ghost story by flashlight.

142. Keep Lifesavers in your pocket.

143. Do card tricks.

144. Buy the kids their own tool sets.

145. If they don't like a sport, don't insist they play it.

146. Not *every* boy your daughter dates is pond scum.

147. Play leap frog.

148. Teach them to somersault.

149. Hang out in their treehouse only when invited.

150. Teach them the importance of a firm handshake.

151. If you have a dimple, make sure your son inherits it.

152. Read them *Lord of the Rings*.

153. Explain what it is you do all day at work.

154. Ask them what they did at school today.

155. Take them for a ride in a wheelbarrow.

156. Take them into your office for a visit.

157. Build them a go-cart.

158. Take them sledding.

159. Take them fly fishing.

160. Put on a puppet show.

161. Throw a game so they're the winner.

162. Be extemporaneous.

163. Teach them how to look up words like extemporaneous in the dictionary.

164. Take them on a tour of a battleship.

165. Chase your toddler around the dining room table.

166. Help the kids look through a microscope.

167. Put your arm under baby's tummy and help her "fly."

168. When everything's on the floor, have a "pick-up party."

169. Study a martial art with them.

170. Show up for pediatrician visits.

171. Even Homer Simpson has some good qualities.

172. Don't kiss the baby when your beard's all stubbly.

173. (But feel free to kiss Mommy anytime.)

174. Anniversary dinners are not picked up at the drive-through window.

175. Forget Mother's Day and you're in the doghouse.

176. If it's broken, fix it.

177. If you can't fix it, buy a new one.

178. If you can't afford a new one, buy a used one.

179. If you can't afford a used one, it's time to ask for a raise.

180. Show them how much *fun* it is to mow the lawn.

181. Admit it, you like the suburbs more than you expected.

182. Teach your daughter how to pump her own gas.

183. Teach her to fix a flat tire.

184. Be strong enough to show your weak spots.

185. Be brave enough to say when you're afraid.

186. Be wise enough to say you don't know all the answers.

187. Don't wear a tool belt unless you're willing to fix something.

188. No couch potatoes please.

189. Arrange a camp-out in the back yard.

190. Explore.

191. Be reasonable.

192. Try to be fair even when life isn't.

193. Remember, you too were an adolescent smart aleck.

194. Remember, you too were a party animal.

195. Let them have a pet.

196. Let them have a chemistry set.

197. No one ever said fatherhood was for the faint-hearted.

198. Once you have children you'll never need an alarm clock.

199. No matter how big your house is, it keeps seeming smaller.

200. No matter how many books you've read, parenthood is a shock.

201. Don't look now but they get cuter every day.

202. You'll feel proud when they give a hearty burp.

203. You'll feel mortified when they snub you for their toy bear.

204. Father's intuition is just as valid as mother's intuition.

205. Put your baby on your chest and synchronize your breathing.

206. Don't believe everything you read.

207. Learn to shop by catalogue.

208. When your kid smiles at you, you're putty.

209. "Ask your mother" is a cop-out.

210. Buy an idiot-proof camera.

211. Buy film in bulk.

212. Remember, your generation started the sexual revolution.

213. For a good laugh, show your kids your old "hip" clothes.

214. Watch both versions of *Father of the Bride.*

215. Sneak into their room and watch them sleep.

216. Take them to get their hair cut.

217. Play miniature golf.

218. Extend a business trip and take along the family.

219. You *will* go to Disneyworld so you may as well enjoy it.

220. Yes, you should charge them rent when they have a full-time job.

221. No, you can't charge them rent when they're still in grade school.

222. Make sure their seat belts are buckled.

223. Wear the ties they buy.

224. Let them read your car magazines.

225. Tell them about when the dinosaurs roamed.

226. (Assure them you don't remember this *personally*.)

227. Tell them a baseball "strike" used to mean the batter swung and missed.

228. Play geography games with them.

229. Memorize five fun car songs.

230. Prioritize.

231. Learn who's who on *Sesame Street*.

232. Don't tell them Barney's just a guy in a purple suit.

233. Tell a riddle.

234. Say a tongue twister.

235. Learn how to make balloon animals.

236. Make shadow animals with your hands.

237. Take your kids to the driving range with you.

238. Your teenagers are *supposed* to knock you off your pedestal.

239. No matter what, your daughter will always be your little girl.

240. When your son turns sixteen, take a photo of your car to remember it by.

241. Teach them the rules of the road.

242. Say a prayer for their Driver's Ed instructor.

243. Dress up and take your daughter to a fancy restaurant.

244. Discipline is not the same as punishment.

245. You've got to draw the line somewhere.

246. Only set rules that are enforceable.

247. (And don't forget to enforce them.)

248. If your daughter's acting weird, blame estrogen.

249. If your son's acting weird, blame testosterone.

250. If your wife's acting weird, blame the kids.

251. If you're acting weird, join the club.

252. Two-year-olds don't believe in gravity unless they're Isaac Newton.

253. Thirteen is too young to sign them up for the Army.

254. Thirteen is too old to stick a pacifier in their mouth.

255. Tell them you believe in miracles.

256. Try a turn-off-the-T.V. week and see what happens.

257. Hey, if public school was good enough for you . . .

258. Play peek-a-boo and patty-cake.

259. Get them that set of blocks that inspired Frank Lloyd Wright.

260. Hoisting toddlers builds upper body strength.

261. If you'd had a lower sperm count, you could be relaxing right now.

262. Well, at least you've done your bit for survival of the species.

263. Don't name your child anything with a Roman numeral after it.

264. Face it: your one year old thinks you're a trampoline.

265. Remember: when they're grounded, you're grounded.

266. Just because you hate the circus is no reason to deprive them.

267. Don't look now, but all your kids can forge your signature.

268. Don't look now, but they've memorized your Visa number.

269. Don't look now but they know the password to the school computer system.

270. Murphy must have known your kids when he invented his law.

271. Yours is a noble calling.

272. It hurts when you write their whole term paper and get a B minus.

273. See if you can get their child psychiatrist to prescribe a nice tranquilizer for you.

274. If you think your kids dress stupid, look at your photos from the '70s.

275. Your son won't borrow your clothes but your daughter will.

276. You can't have too much Old Spice.

277. Your kids will never think you're hip but your grandkids just might.

278. Attempt to put the gas grill together.

279. Help them earn a merit badge.

280. Update the family photos in your wallet.

281. Get a sports star's autograph "for the kids."

282. Trade tips with other dads on the Internet.

283. *Somebody's* got to wash out the diaper pail.

284. Review your life insurance policy every so often.

285. Make sure you have an up-to-date will.

286. You too can be a pinball wizard.

287. Who says you can't cry over spilt milk?

288. Give the babysitter a lift home.

289. Do not give the babysitter a kiss good-night.

290. Know when to say you're sorry.

291. Listen carefully.

292. Follow through.

293. Read them *Good Night Moon*—again.

294. The only thing worse than your puberty is theirs.

295. Your teens are *supposed* to look mortified when you're around.

296. When they say "My old man," they mean *you*.

297. Make friends with an orthodontist.

298. Make friends with a college admissions officer.

299. Keep the key to the liquor cabinet on your key ring.

300. If you want to know what your kids are doing when you're out, watch *Risky Business*.

301. Never say, "Hey, is that *acne?*"

302. Say the hand-made cufflinks are what you always wanted.

303. Be a proud papa.

304. You know your daughter's growing up when she makes you blush.

305. You know your son's growing up when your wife makes him blush.

306. Don't get into a rut.

307. Bet your own dad seems pretty smart by now.

308. Bet your granddad seems like a *genius*.

309. Hang tough when your son misses the field goal.

310. It's natural to have mixed feelings when they say they want to be just like you.

311. Take half a Xanax before you look at their report cards.

312. Take a whole Xanax before you look at their SAT scores.

313. Take two Xanax when they get a nose ring.

314. The playground is a good place to bond with other dads.

315. Tell them about your heroes.

316. Tell them about the turning points in your life.

317. Tell them what you wish you'd done differently.

318. Tell them what you'd do the same all over again.

319. Tell them how much they mean to you.

320. Help plan campaign strategy when they run for student council.

321. On the bright side: arguing with them helps them hone their skills for the debate team.

322. Take a list to the supermarket instead of improvising.

323. Keep some emergency cash in the house.

324. Know where the First Aid kit is.

325. Learn the Heimlich maneuver.

326. Face it: hanging Christmas lights is a competitive sport.

327. Know the names of all your daughter's dolls.

328. Know the names of the Power Rangers.

329. The cost of private kindergarten is what?

330. "Mom said we could . . ." is best corroborated with Mom.

331. Sometimes it's best not to ask for too many details.

332. Sometimes it's best not to ask.

333. Practice saying, "Can't you call your mother once in a while?"

334. Practice saying, "Don't break your mother's heart."

335. Wear a rain slicker when you bathe the baby.

336. You can't leave Baby Gap without buying something.

337. In fact, you can't leave Baby Gap without buying *everything*.

338. Learn to make a mean macaroni and cheese.

339. Learn to love tuna melts.

340. Memorize their favorite ice cream flavors.

341. Run for a seat on the school board.

342. Make fudge.

343. Learn to tackle minor sewing repairs.

344. Trust us: there are *three* teaspoons in a tablespoon.

345. Have "target practice" with your two-year-old toilet trainee.

346. Include pictures of your kids in your Christmas cards.

347. Learn to take temperatures.

348. Accidents happen.

349. Don't take colic personally.

350. Tell them why you chose their name and what it means.

351. Be kind to their animals.

352. (Even the stuffed ones.)

353. Don't offer to do their chores for them.

354. Let them be your caddies.

355. Display all their trophies and awards prominently.

356. Memorize some of Tim Allen's lines.

357. Reassure your wife she's a good mother.

358. Don't let them know quite how much you worry.

359. Think young.

360. Think fast.

361. Every once in a while take your wife away from it all.

362. The things they will never remember are the things you always will.

363. The things you forget are the things they'll tell their therapist.

364. Deep down, you're such a softie.

365. Take care of yourself—your family is counting on you.